Simple Salsa Recipes

GOLDEN WEST PUBLISHERS

Cover photo © 1997 Walter Urie/Westlight

ISBN #1-885590-25-3

Printed in the United States of America

Copyright © 1997 by Golden West Publishers. All rights reserved. This book or any portion thereof may not be reproduced in any form, except for review purposes, without the written permission of the publisher.

Information in this book is deemed to be authentic and accurate by publisher. However, publisher disclaims any liability incurred in connection with the use of information appearing in this book.

Golden West Publishers, Inc.
4113 N. Longview Ave.
Phoenix, AZ 85014, USA
(602) 265-4392

Table of Contents

Table Salsa	7
Salsa de Chile Verde	8
Zesty Quick Salsa	9
Spicy Salsa	10
Salsa de Chile Verde con Queso	11
Basic Cheese Sauce	12
Enchilada Sauce with Cheese	13
Salsa Sabrosa	14
Avocado Sauce	15
Tomato Enchilada Sauce	16
Quick Salsa for Two	17
Taco Salsa	17
Salsa Picante	18
Hamburger Salsa	19
Green Chile Relish	20
Salsas #1 — #5	21-24
Cilantro Salsa	25

- All-Purpose Salsa 26
- Everyday Salsa 26
- Easy Salsa 27
- Fresh Salsa 28
- Salsa for a Crowd 29
- Barbecue Salsa 30
- Black Bean Salsa 31
- Chili Powder Salsa 32
- Cucumber & Radish Salsa 33
- Easy Salsa Rojo 34
- Fresh Vegetable Salsa 35
- Herbed Salsa for Chicken 36
- Honey Salsa 37
- Lime Salsa 38
- Madera Salsa 39
- Mango Salsa 40
- Pico de Gallo #1 – #3 41-42
- Rellenos Salsa 43
- Salsa Crema for Omelets 44

Salsa for Baked Fish 45
Salsa for Shrimp 46
Salsa Verde 47
Steak Salsa 48
Sunflower Salsa 49
Sweet Spicy Salsa 50
Tequila Salsa 51
Tomatillo Salsa 52
Wine Salsa for Baked Ham 53
Yellow Fruit Salsa for Fish 54
Yellow Chile Salsa 55
Crookneck Squash Salsa 56
Avocado Salsa 57
Creamy Avocado Salsa 58
Salsa for Mixed Salad Greens 59
Herb Salsa for Salads 60
Salsa for Fruit Salad 61
Orange Peach & Orange Salsas 62

Salsa

(SAHL-sah) The Mexican word for "sauce," which can signify either cooked or fresh mixtures. Salsas range in spiciness from mild to mouth-searing.

Salsas should be kept in tightly covered bowls or jars and may be refrigerated for 6 or 7 days.

Table Salsa

4 whole TOMATOES, chopped
1 JALAPEÑO, chopped
1/2 small ONION, chopped
1 can (6 oz.) TOMATO PASTE
1 CHILTEPIN, minced
1/2 clove GARLIC
1/4 tsp. PEPPER
1/2 tsp. SALT
1/4 tsp. PAPRIKA
1 Tbsp. VINEGAR

Mix all ingredients, adding seasonings last, in a blender. Blend until mixture reaches desired thickness. Can be refrigerated up to a week in closed glass container.

Salsa de Chile Verde
(Green Chile Salsa)

3 to 4 TOMATOES, chopped
2 Tbsp. chopped ONION
1 can (4 oz.) diced GREEN CHILES
1/2 tsp. SALT
1/4 tsp. coarsely ground PEPPER
2 dried CILANTRO LEAVES, crushed

Combine all ingredients. This is a mild table salsa that goes with everything!

Zesty Quick Salsa

1 thick ring of ONION, diced
3 small STEWED TOMATOES, chopped
1 can (4 oz.) diced GREEN CHILES
3 Tbsp. TOMATO PASTE
1/8 tsp. GARLIC POWDER
SALT and PEPPER to taste

Combine onions, tomatoes and chiles in a saucepan and bring to a boil. Add 1 tablespoon tomato paste and stir. Add 2 more tablespoons of tomato paste. Add seasonings. Reduce heat, cover and let simmer 10 minutes, stirring occasionally. Makes 1 medium-sized bowl of salsa.

Spicy Salsa

1 thick ring of ONION, chopped
3 whole stewed TOMATOES, chopped
1 JALAPEÑO, diced
2 oz. TOMATO PURÉE
2 oz. diced GREEN CHILES
dash GARLIC POWDER
SALT and PEPPER to taste

Mix all ingredients in blender until thoroughly combined. Makes 1 1/2 cups salsa. Refrigerate for up to a week in covered glass container.

Salsa de Chile Verde con Queso
(Salsa with Green Chiles and Cheese)

1 tsp. OIL
4 to 5 fresh TOMATOES, chopped
1 can (7 oz.) diced GREEN CHILES
2 Tbsp. diced ONIONS
dash GARLIC POWDER
SALT and PEPPER to taste
1 can (6 oz.) TOMATO SAUCE
1/2 cup shredded LONGHORN CHEESE

In a saucepan, heat oil and sauté tomatoes, chiles and onions. Stir in garlic powder, salt and pepper, tomato sauce and cheese. Add water in small amounts to desired thickness. Serve hot or cold. Makes 6 servings.

Basic Cheese Sauce

2 cups LONGHORN CHEESE, grated
6 Tbsp. OLIVE OIL
1/4 tsp. SALT
1/4 tsp. PEPPER
1/2 tsp. PAPRIKA
1 can (4 oz.) diced GREEN CHILES
1 Tbsp. VINEGAR
5 Tbsp. EVAPORATED MILK

Melt cheese in hot oil and add seasonings. Add chiles, vinegar and milk slowly while stirring. Heat to a bubbly boil. Makes 3/4 cup.

Enchilada Sauce with Cheese

3 Tbsp. OIL
3 Tbsp. FLOUR
6 Tbsp. CHILI POWDER
2 cups WATER (or meat stock)
1 tsp. SALT
1/2 tsp. GARLIC POWDER
1/2 cup CHEDDAR CHEESE

In a saucepan, heat oil and brown flour. Dissolve chili powder in water and add to flour, mixing well. Add seasonings and blend. Bring to a bubbly boil, stirring frequently. Add cheese, cover and simmer 5 minutes. Makes 1 1/4 cups sauce.

Salsa Sabrosa

(Savory Salsa)

4 stewed TOMATOES, chopped
3 Tbsp. TOMATO PASTE
4 CHILTEPINS, crushed
1 can (4 oz.) diced GREEN CHILES
1 tbsp. diced ONION
2 tsp. VINEGAR
1/4 tsp. SALT
1/8 tsp. ground PEPPER
1/8 tsp. ground CUMIN
1/8 tsp. GARLIC POWDER
1 tsp. fresh-dried, crushed CILANTRO

Put tomatoes and tomato paste in blender and mix. Add chiles, onion and vinegar and mix. Add balance of ingredients and blend until smooth and thick. Makes 1 1/2 cups.

Avocado Sauce

2 Tbsp. LEMON or LIME JUICE
4 Tbsp. EVAPORATED MILK
1 tsp. DRY MUSTARD
1/2 tsp. SALT
dash GARLIC SALT
PEPPER
1 Tbsp. minced PIMENTOS
1 cup mashed AVOCADOS

In a blender, combine juice, milk and seasonings and blend well. Add avocados. Mix for desired thickness. Makes 1 1/2 cups sauce.

Tomato Enchilada Sauce

2 1/2 cups TOMATO SAUCE
1 Tbsp. TOMATO PASTE
1/4 cup WATER
2 Tbsp. diced ONION
pinch ground CUMIN
1/8 tsp. GARLIC POWDER
1/4 tsp. GROUND PEPPER
1 can (4 oz.) diced GREEN CHILES
SALT to taste

Combine ingredients in a saucepan. Heat to a bubbly boil, reduce heat, simmer 10 to 15 minutes. Stir frequently. Makes 2 1/2 cups.

Quick Salsa for Two

2 Tbsp. SALAD OIL
2 Tbsp. diced ONION
1 clove GARLIC, minced
1/2 tsp. SALT

dash CAYENNE PEPPER
4 stewed TOMATOES, chopped
1 can (7 oz.) diced GREEN CHILES

Heat oil and sauté onions. Add balance of ingredients.

Taco Salsa

4 to 5 STEWED TOMATOES, chopped
1 can (4 oz.) diced GREEN CHILES
2 Tbsp. diced ONION

1/4 tsp. SALT
1/2 tsp. OREGANO
dash GARLIC POWDER

Combine all ingredients in a bowl and mix thoroughly.

Salsa Picante

(Spicy Salsa)

2 Tbsp. diced ONION
2 tsp. SALAD OIL
1 can (4 oz.) diced GREEN CHILES
2 JALAPEÑOS, diced
3 Tbsp. TOMATO PASTE
SALT and PEPPER to taste
1 tsp. VINEGAR

In a saucepan, sauté onion in oil. Add green chiles and jalapeños. Cook for 2 minutes over medium heat, stirring frequently. Add tomato paste and stir in seasonings. (If salsa is too hot, add 1 teaspoon vinegar.) Stir, cover, and cook for 5 minutes. Uncover and simmer for 5 minutes. Makes one bowl of salsa.

Hamburger Salsa

1 Tbsp. OIL
2 Tbsp. diced ONION
1 can (7 oz.) diced GREEN CHILES
1 small JALAPEÑO, diced
1 can (6 oz.) TOMATO SAUCE
2 Tbsp. TOMATO PASTE
1 cup cooked GROUND BEEF, drained

Sauté onions in oil. Add chiles, tomato sauce and paste. Stir and bring to a boil. Cover and cook over medium heat 5 to 8 minutes. Add seasonings, simmer 5 minutes. Add meat and heat thoroughly. Makes a great dip with tortilla chips.

Green Chile Relish

1 lb. fresh GREEN CHILES
1/4 cup VINEGAR
1/2 tsp. SALT
1/4 cup WATER
2 Tbsp. CORN OIL

Wash chiles and remove stems and seeds (use kitchen gloves!) Coarsely grind chiles in food grinder. Combine all ingredients in a saucepan. Cook slowly over medium heat for 20 minutes, stirring occasionally. Cool in glass bowl or jar in refrigerator before serving.

Salsa #1

2 cups peeled and chopped TOMATOES
1 stalk CELERY, diced
1 ONION, diced
1 GREEN BELL PEPPER, diced
1 1/2 tsp. SALT
1 Tbsp. VINEGAR
1 Tbsp. SUGAR
1 can (4 oz.) diced GREEN CHILES

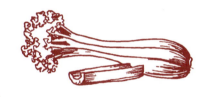

Combine all ingredients and blend well. For a finer texture, run through a food grinder using a fine blade. Cover tightly in glass bowl or jar and chill overnight.

Salsa #2

1 can (16 oz.) diced TOMATOES
1 can (4 oz.) diced GREEN CHILES
2 medium ONIONS
2 cloves GARLIC
1 Tbsp. CHILI POWDER
1/2 tsp. SALT
coarsely ground PEPPER
1 Tbsp. WHITE VINEGAR

    Combine all ingredients in a glass bowl, cover and refrigerate overnight.

Salsa #3

1 can (4 oz.) diced GREEN CHILES
4 medium TOMATOES, peeled and diced
1/4 cup sliced GREEN ONIONS
1 tsp. SALT

In a blender, combine all ingredients and blend until very smooth. Place in a covered glass bowl or jar and refrigerate.

Salsa #4

1 can (16 oz.) crushed TOMATOES   **2 Tbsp. VINEGAR**
1 can (4 oz.) diced GREEN CHILES   **2 Tbsp. OIL**

Combine all ingredients. Place in covered glass bowl or jar and refrigerate.

Salsa #5

1 can (16 oz.) crushed TOMATOES
1 can (4 oz.) diced GREEN CHILES
1 ONION, chopped
2 cloves GARLIC, crushed
1 Tbsp. CHILI POWDER
1/2 tsp. CUMIN
1/2 tsp. SALT
1 Tbsp. WHITE VINEGAR

Combine all ingredients and mix thoroughly. Place in covered glass bowl or jar in refrigerator for several hours.

Cilantro Salsa

**4 med. TOMATOES, diced
1 sm. ONION, diced
1 GREEN BELL PEPPER, diced
1 can (4 oz.) diced GREEN CHILES, drained
1/2 tsp. dried OREGANO
1/4 tsp. SALT
1/2 cup fresh CILANTRO (or 1 Tbsp. dried)
1 Tbsp. ORANGE JUICE**

Combine all ingredients in medium bowl. Serve chilled or at room temperature. Makes 2 cups.

All-Purpose Salsa

4 cups TOMATOES, chopped
2 Tbsp. diced GREEN CHILES
1 1/2 tsp. LEMON JUICE

1 1/2 tsp. VEGETABLE OIL
1 tsp. dried OREGANO

Combine all ingredients and mix well. Serve at room temperature or refrigerate. Makes 1 1/2 cups.

Everyday Salsa

5 lg. TOMATOES, chopped
1/2 bunch CILANTRO, chopped
1/3 cup GREEN ONION, chopped

1 1/2 Tbsp. LIME JUICE
SALT and PEPPER to taste

Combine all ingredients and mix thoroughly. Serve at room temperature or refrigerate. Makes 3 cups.

Easy Salsa

1 can (16 oz.) crushed TOMATOES
1 can (4 oz.) diced GREEN CHILES, undrained
1/2 tsp. GARLIC SALT
1/2 tsp. OREGANO
1/2 tsp. dried CILANTRO
1/4 tsp. CHILI POWDER

Combine tomatoes and chiles and mix well. Stir in spices and herbs and again mix well. Can be stored in refrigerator for several days. Makes 2 1/2 cups.

Fresh Salsa

5 med. TOMATOES, chopped
1 GREEN BELL PEPPER, minced
1/2 cup minced ONION
1 clove GARLIC, pressed
4 sm. GREEN CHILES
1/2 tsp. fresh, snipped OREGANO

Remove stems and seeds from chiles and chop fine. (May substitute 1 tsp. dried oregano for fresh.) Combine all ingredients and mix well. Makes 2 cups.

Salsa for a Crowd

3 cans (28 oz.) STEWED TOMATOES
1 can (15 oz.) TOMATO SAUCE
3 med. fresh TOMATOES, diced
3 bunches GREEN ONIONS, chopped
1 Tbsp. canned, chopped JALAPEÑOS
2 cloves GARLIC, pressed
1 bunch fresh CILANTRO, chopped
1 can (7 oz.) diced GREEN CHILES
1 tsp. SUGAR

Combine all ingredients and store in glass jars in refrigerator for up to a week. Makes 6 cups.

Barbecue Salsa

1 cup MAYONNAISE
1 cup bottled CHILI SAUCE
2 Tbsp. WORCESTERSHIRE SAUCE
3 Tbsp. CRUSHED RED PEPPERS, from jar
GARLIC SALT to taste

Mix all ingredients together and brush on ribs while cooking. Makes 2 cups.

Black Bean Salsa

1 can (15 oz.) BLACK BEANS, drained
1 Tbsp. OIL
1/2 cup diced PIMENTOS
1/8 tsp. ground CUMIN
1/2 cup fresh, chopped CILANTRO
4 GREEN ONIONS, diced
1 Tbsp. LIME JUICE

Combine all ingredients and refrigerate until well chilled. This salsa is especially good with chicken and pork. Makes 2/12 cups.

Chili Powder Salsa

2 Tbsp. VEGETABLE OIL
1/2 cup diced ONION
2 cloves GARLIC, crushed
1 can (15 oz.) ITALIAN PLUM TOMATOES, drained and chopped
1/2 tsp. ground CUMIN
1/2 tsp. dried PARSLEY FLAKES
2 tsp. RED CHILI POWDER

Sauté onions and garlic in oil until golden brown. Add remaining ingredients and simmer for 15 minutes. Makes 2 cups.

Cucumber & Radish Salsa

2 cans (13 oz. ea.) TOMATILLOS, drained and diced
1/4 cup diced ONION
1 CUCUMBER, peeled and coarsely chopped
10 RADISHES, quartered
1 SERRANO or JALAPEÑO CHILE, seeded and diced
1 can (4 oz.) diced GREEN CHILES

Combine all ingredients in a glass bowl and chill. Makes 4 cups.

Easy Salsa Rojo

1/4 cup VEGETABLE OIL
1/3 cup FLOUR
2 3/4 cups WATER
1 pkg. (1 oz.) dried RED CHILES, powdered

Heat oil, slowly sprinkle in flour, whisking constantly until all flour is absorbed. Slowly add water, stirring constantly until mixture is smooth and the consistency of gravy. Slowly sprinkle in chile powder, blending completely. Serve over enchiladas, burritos or grilled steak. Makes 3 cups.

Fresh Vegetable Salsa

4 TOMATOES, diced
1 ZUCCHINI SQUASH, diced
1 YELLOW SQUASH, diced
1 sm. jar diced PIMENTOS, drained
2 sm. JALAPEÑO or SERRANO CHILES, diced
2 Tbsp. OLIVE OIL
2 Tbsp. LIME JUICE
1/3 cup fresh, chopped CILANTRO

Combine all ingredients and mix well. Cover and refrigerate overnight. Serve as a relish. Makes 2 cups.

Herbed Salsa for Chicken

3 Tbsp. OLIVE OIL
2 Tbsp. LEMON JUICE
1 tsp. ONION SALT
2 Tsp. canned diced JALAPEÑO, reserve juice
1 tsp. dried BASIL
1/4 tsp. ROSEMARY

Combine oil, juice, salt, jalapeño and 1 tablespoonful of jalapeño juice. Brush on chicken before baking or grilling. Serve remaining salsa warm as a table salsa. Makes 1/2 cup.

Honey Salsa

4 Tbsp. VEGETABLE OIL
4 Tbsp. LIME JUICE
2 Tbsp. HONEY
3 lg. fresh TOMATOES, diced
1 JALAPEÑO or SERRANO CHILE, minced
1 Tbsp. fresh, chopped CILANTRO (or 2 tsp. dried CILANTRO)

Blend all ingredients together and serve with grilled chicken. Makes 1 1/4 cups.

Lime Salsa

2 lg. TOMATOES, diced
2 lg. TOMATILLOS, husked and diced
1/3 cup diced RED ONION
1/3 cup diced BELL PEPPER
2 Tbsp. fresh LIME JUICE
2 tsp. grated LIME PEEL

Mix together all ingredients. Cover and refrigerate several hours or overnight. Makes 2 cups.

Madera Salsa

3 tbsp. VEGETABLE OIL
1 BELL PEPPER, chopped
1 lg. ONION, chopped
2 CARROTS, chopped
4 stalks CELERY, chopped
1 can (28 oz.) crushed TOMATOES, undrained
1 can (7 oz.) diced GREEN CHILES
1/4 tsp. SUGAR
2 tsp. RED CHILE POWDER (or 3 tsp. commercial CHILI POWDER)
1/4 tsp. ground CUMIN
1/2 tsp. dried CILANTRO

Sauté bell pepper, onion, carrots and celery in oil until bell peppers begin to blister. Slowly add all remaining ingredients, beginning with the tomatoes. Simmer slowly 1 hour. Makes 4 cups.

Mango Salsa

1 MANGO, peeled and diced
2 Tbsp. canned JALAPEÑOS, diced
1/2 cup diced ONION
1/4 cup LIME JUICE
1 Tbsp. dried CILANTRO
1/4 tsp. dried CUMIN

Combine all ingredients and refrigerate several hours. Serve with fish. Makes 1 cup.

Pico de Gallo #1

**6 GREEN ONIONS, chopped
(include green tops)
2 to 3 JALAPEÑOS, seeded
and chopped**

**4 med. TOMATOES, chopped
1 1/2 Tbsp. VEGETABLE OIL
1/3 cup fresh, chopped
CILANTRO**

Blend all ingredients, stir well and chill.   Makes 2 cups.

Pico de Gallo #2

**1 1/2 cups diced and seeded
WATERMELON
1 cup peeled and diced JICAMA
1 ORANGE, peeled and diced**

**1 JALAPEÑO, seeded and diced
3 Tbsp. fresh, chopped CILANTRO
1 Tbsp. LIME JUICE**

Blend all ingredients, stir well and chill.   Makes 3 cups.

Pico de Gallo #3

4 lg. TOMATOES, chopped
1/4 cup chopped ONION
1/4 cup peeled and chopped CUCUMBER
2 Tbsp. canned JALAPEÑO, diced
1 Tbsp. LIME JUICE
sprinkle of GARLIC SALT
2 Tbsp. fresh, chopped CILANTRO

Mix all ingredients and chill. Makes 2 1/2 cups.

Pico de Gallo *[PEE-koh day GI-yoh] Spanish for "rooster's beak", is a relish made of finely chopped ingredients like jícama, oranges, onions, bell peppers, jalapeño peppers and cucumbers, along with various seasonings.*

Rellenos Salsa

2 Tbsp. VEGETABLE OIL
2 Tbsp. minced ONION
1 cup STEWED TOMATOES
1 can (8 oz.) TOMATO SAUCE
1 CHICKEN BOUILLON CUBE
1/4 tsp. ground CUMIN
'1/4 tsp. OREGANO flakes

Heat oil and sauté onions. Add remaining ingredients and simmer slowly for 30 minutes. Makes 2 cups (enough for 6 rellenos).

Salsa Crema for Omelets

4 Tbsp. BUTTER
4 Tbsp. FLOUR
1 1/2 cups WHOLE MILK or LIGHT CREAM
1/2 cup diced ONION
1 can (7 oz.) diced GREEN CHILES
1 jar (3 oz.) diced PIMENTOS
1 tsp. dried CILANTRO

Melt butter, stir in flour and blend with whisk until flour is absorbed. Gradually stir in milk (or cream) and stir until thickened. Stir in remaining ingredients. Serve hot, spooned over omelets. Makes 2 cups.

Salsa for Baked Fish

1 Tbsp. VEGETABLE OIL
1 cup ONION, sliced
2 cups chopped TOMATOES
1/2 can (2 oz.) diced GREEN CHILES
2 Tbsp. LEMON JUICE
1 tsp. CAPERS
1 jar (4 oz.) diced PIMENTOS, drained

Heat oil and sauté onions. Add remaining ingredients and simmer 15 minutes. Makes 3 cups.

Salsa for Shrimp

1/3 cup VEGETABLE OIL
3 cloves GARLIC, crushed
1 Tbsp. ground GINGER
2 Tbsp. LEMON JUICE
1 Tbsp. crushed RED CHILES

Sauté garlic in oil until lightly browned. Add balance of ingredients and heat through. Spoon over cooked shrimp. Makes 1/2 cup.

Salsa Verde

1 can (15 oz.) TOMATILLOS, drained
2 JALAPEÑOS, seeded and chopped
1/3 cup chopped ONION
1 tsp. dried CILANTRO
2 Tbsp. VEGETABLE OIL

Combine tomatillos, jalapeños, onion and cilantro in blender. Blend until smooth. Heat oil in small skillet, add blender mixture and sauté lightly. Makes 2 cups.

Steak Salsa

3 JALAPEÑOS, seeded and diced
3 cloves GARLIC, crushed
1/3 cup diced ONION
1 tsp. dried OREGANO (or 2 tsp. fresh OREGANO leaves, chopped)
1/2 tsp. cracked BLACK PEPPER
1/2 cup OLIVE OIL
1/2 cup RED WINE
1 Tbsp. LIME JUICE

Mix all ingredients and store in covered glass jar in refrigerator for 24 hours before serving. Makes 2 cups.

Sunflower Salsa

1 cup shelled SUNFLOWER SEEDS
1 Tbsp. OIL
1/4 tsp. CLOVES
1/2 tsp. CINNAMON
2 tsp. ground CHILI POWDER
1 tsp. COCOA
sprinkle of GARLIC SALT
1 Tbsp. WHITE WINE
1 cup WATER or STOCK

Sauté seeds in oil over medium heat until lightly toasted. Combine balance of ingredients (reserve 1/2 cup water or stock) in blender and blend until smooth. Simmer mixture over medium heat, adding reserved liquid until slightly thickened. Makes 1 1/2 cups.

Sweet Spicy Salsa

2 med. ONIONS, chopped
2 cloves GARLIC, crushed
2 Tbsp. BUTTER
1 can (15 oz.) TOMATO SAUCE
1 can (8 oz.) TOMATO SAUCE
1/2 cup BROWN SUGAR
1 Tbsp. CHILI POWDER
1/2 tsp. INSTANT COFFEE
1/2 tsp. DRY MUSTARD
1/4 tsp. TABASCO®
1/4 tsp. liquid SMOKE
2 CHICKEN BOUILLON CUBES
1/2 cup LIME JUICE

In a skillet, sauté onion and garlic in butter. Add balance of ingredients and simmer slowly for 1 hour. Makes 3 cups.

Tequila Salsa

1/2 cup OLIVE OIL
1/2 cup LIME JUICE
1/2 cup TEQUILA
2 Tbsp. TRIPLE SEC
1 can (4 oz.) diced GREEN CHILES, undrained

Combine all ingredients. Use as a marinade for chicken or turkey, or store in refrigerator in covered glass jar to use as a side dish.

Tomatillo Salsa

1 can (13 oz.) TOMATILLOS, drained and diced
1 can (4 oz.) seeded and diced JALAPEÑO CHILES
1/4 cup minced ONION
1/2 tsp. dried LEMON PEEL
1/2 tsp. WHITE SUGAR
1 Tbsp. dried CILANTRO, crushed

Combine all ingredients and refrigerate for several hours. Makes 1 1/2 cups.

Wine Salsa for Baked Ham

1 1/2 cups PORT
1/2 cup SUGAR (white or light brown)
1/2 tsp. LEMON PEEL
1/2 tsp. ORANGE PEEL
1 JALAPEÑO CHILE, minced

Heat all ingredients, simmering gently. Serve hot with baked ham. Makes 1 1/2 cups.

Yellow Fruit Salsa for Fish

1 can (15 oz.) TOMATOES, drained
1 can (8 1/4 oz.) PINEAPPLE chunks, drained
1 cup PAPAYA, peeled and diced
1 JALAPEÑO, seeded and diced
2 Tbsp. LIME JUICE

Combine all ingredients in a glass bowl. Cover and refrigerate for several hours. Serve with your favorite fish. Makes 3 cups.

Yellow Chile Salsa

5 YELLOW WAX CHILES
1 JALAPEÑO CHILE
1 can (16 oz.) stewed TOMATOES
1 GREEN ONION, minced
1/4 tsp. OREGANO
1/4 tsp. GARLIC POWDER
SALT to taste

Roast chiles, wrap in damp cloth and steam. Peel and remove seeds. Place roasted and peeled chiles and remaining ingredients in blender and blend until smooth. Makes 2 cups.

Crookneck Squash Salsa

2 uncooked and diced YELLOW CROOKNECK SQUASH
1/4 cup diced ONION
1/4 cup YELLOW BELL PEPPER
1 can (15 oz.) TOMATOES and GREEN CHILES, drained and diced
1 JALAPEÑO CHILE, seeded and diced
1/4 tsp. ground CUMIN

Combine all ingredients and chill for several hours. Makes 2 cups.

Avocado Salsa

2 lg. ripe AVOCADOS
1 lg. TOMATO, chopped
1 Tbsp. diced GREEN CHILES
1 Tbsp. diced ONION
1 Tbsp. CILANTRO, chopped
2 Tbsp. WHITE WINE

Mash avocados, stir in remaining ingredients. Serve over salads as a dressing. Makes 1 1/2 cups.

Creamy Avocado Salsa

1 lg. AVOCADO, diced
1/2 cup SOUR CREAM
1 clove GARLIC, crushed
1 tsp. dried CILANTRO, crushed
1 tsp. TABASCO®
2 Tbsp. LIME JUICE

Combine all ingredients in blender. Serve well chilled over salad. Makes 1 1/2 cups.

Salsa for Mixed Salad Greens

1 cup OLIVE OIL
3 tsp. DIJON MUSTARD
4 Tbsp. WINE VINEGAR
1/4 tsp. SALT
1/4 tsp. CRACKED PEPPER

Combine all ingredients and beat well with wire whisk. Toss with chilled greens. Makes 1 1/2 cups.

Herb Salsa for Salads

1 cup OLIVE OIL
2 Tbsp. LIME JUICE
3 Tbsp. BASIL VINEGAR
1 tsp. dried OREGANO
1/4 tsp. GARLIC SALT
1/4 tsp. PEPPER
1 jar (3 oz.) diced PIMENTOS
2 shakes dried LEMON PEEL
1 tsp. SUGAR

Place all ingredients in a blender and blend until smooth. Refrigerate several hours. Makes 1 1/2 cups.

Salsa for Fruit Salad

2 Tbsp. OLIVE OIL
2 Tbsp. VINEGAR
1/2 cup SOUR CREAM
1 tsp. LEMON JUICE
1 tsp. SUGAR
1/2 tsp. ground CUMIN
2 Tbsp. MINT LEAVES, chopped
2 Tbsp. fresh CILANTRO, chopped

Combine all ingredients and mix well. Chill for several hours. Makes 1 1/4 cups.

Orange Salsa

1/4 cup ORANGE JUICE
3 cups ORANGE MARMALADE
1 1/2 tsp. LEMON JUICE
3 Tbsp. BUTTER
1/2 cup ORANGE LIQUEUR

Combine all ingredients in a saucepan and simmer for 15 minutes. Serve warm over cake or ice cream. Makes 2 cups salsa.

Orange Peach Salsa

1 cup PEACH PRESERVES
1/2 cup ORANGE JUICE
3 Tbsp. GRAND MARNIER

Heat preserves and juice in a saucepan, stirring constantly until preserves are melted. Cool slightly and stir in Grand Marnier. Makes 1 cup salsa.

Simply Sensational™ Cook Books

GOLDEN WEST PUBLISHERS

"Mini-sized" cookbooks packed with savory recipes! Give your tastebuds a treat with authentic recipes that are both flavorful and easy to make. These books are great for personal use and make wonderful gifts!

Each attractive 5 1/2" x 4" book has 64 pages and is comb bound for lay flat use. All books only $4.95 each!

For a free catalog of Golden West cookbooks call 1-800-658-5830